THE LIBRARY OF WEAPONS OF MASS DESTRUCTION™

Terrorism, Dirty Bombs, *and* Weapons *of* Mass Destruction

JASON PORTERFIELD

The Rosen Publishing Group, Inc., New York

Published in 2005 by The Rosen Publishing Group, Inc.
29 East 21st Street, New York, NY 10010

Library of Congress Cataloging-in-Publication Data
Porterfield, Jason.
Terrorism, dirty bombs, and weapons of mass destruction / by Jason
Porterfield.—1st ed.
    p. cm.— (The library of weapons of mass destruction)
Includes bibliographical references and index.
ISBN 1-4042-0291-9 (library binding)
1. Terrorism—Juvenile literature. 2. Terrorists—Juvenile literature.
3. Terrorism—Prevention—Juvenile literature. 4. Dirty bombs—
Juvenile literature. 5. Weapons of mass destruction—Juvenile literature.
I. Title. II. Series.
HV6431.P668 2005
363.32—dc22
                                                                    2004010821

Manufactured in the United States of America

On the cover: Firefighters drag dummy victims from the scene of a
mock dirty-bomb attack during a drill in Cambridge, Massachusetts, on
May 16, 2004.

[CONTENTS]

INTRODUCTION

On September 11, 2001, terrorists crashed planes into the World Trade Center in New York City and the Pentagon near Washington, D.C. The attack killed more than 2,700 people and destroyed the soaring Twin Towers. People all over the world mourned after the most deadly terrorist attack in history, and the United States sought revenge.

The attacks also weakened America's faith in the government's ability to protect its citizens. During the aftermath, experts set to work analyzing

This view from the Manhattan Bridge shows downtown Manhattan and the Brooklyn Bridge after the September 11, 2001, terrorist attack on the World Trade Center. The successful terrorist strike forced American officials to refocus their attention on preventing the spread of weapons of mass destruction to unfriendly states and particularly to terrorists.

possible intelligence failures and increasing national security. Among other eventualities, authorities began to seriously consider the possibility that terrorists could deploy weapons of mass destruction (WMD), the most lethal weapons known to mankind. If terrorists gain access to WMD, they could then launch an assault even more deadly and destructive than the attack on the World Trade Center.

Terrorism has existed in various forms for thousands of years. The word "terrorism" itself was coined during France's Reign of Terror between 1793 and 1794. During this period, people suspected of

Rescue workers search the enormous wreckage after the collapse of the World Trade Center's Twin Towers on September 11, 2001. Many New York City fire-fighters who participated in the search have developed severe coughs and lung disorders after breathing in the polluted air at the site. Many experts believe that had the terrorists used chemical or biological weapons in the attack, the resulting pollution would have killed and injured far more people than had died that day.

undermining the French Revolution were sent to the guillotine. Since then, the word has taken on a different meaning. Today, it refers to the use of violence against a population or government to bring about change for political or religious reasons.

Throughout much of the twentieth century, terrorists sought to bring attention to their various causes through assassinations, bombings, hijackings, and kidnappings. They wanted their shocking displays of violence to bring attention to their causes, yet they did not want to alienate potential supporters by needlessly killing or harming innocent bystanders.

Kidnappings and hijackings dropped off after the 1970s, as increased security helped deter attempts. The number of terrorist attacks has since decreased further, though the attacks have become more deadly as terrorists have resorted to more violent methods. In some ways, the nature of terrorism has changed as well. Politically motivated terrorist groups once sought to gain sympathy in the public eye by sparing innocent bystanders. However, since the 1980s, religious terrorist groups that view violence against perceived enemies as an end in itself have emerged as a threat to global peace.

The 1995 sarin gas attack on a Tokyo subway by the Japanese doomsday cult Aum Shinrikyo heightened fears that terrorists could gain access to weapons of mass destruction. The use of chemical or biological weapons by a terrorist group could cause waves of illnesses, poisonings, or death among a population, as well as spread fear. An even greater fear is that terrorists may acquire enough radioactive material to construct a so-called dirty bomb for use in a densely populated area.

The global scale of terrorism makes it difficult for governments to keep such weapons out of the hands of terrorists. Some of the materials necessary for these weapons of mass destruction are readily available on the black market or easy for terrorists to manufacture themselves. Others must be stolen or acquired from bribed officials. Today, strengthened security measures and intelligence agents in the United States and abroad work to keep weapons of mass destruction out of the reach of terrorists. ■

1

THE TERRORIST THREAT FROM CHEMICAL AND BIOLOGICAL WEAPONS

Since the end of World War I, advances in weapons technology have led to the development and refinement of weapons of mass destruction. These are weapons capable of indiscriminately killing, injuring, or sickening large numbers of people, rendering an area uninhabitable, and disrupting life for a targeted population.

The phrase "weapons of mass destruction" refers to chemical and biological agents that can be dispersed among a population through the air or water, as well as nuclear and radiological weapons. Many governments have produced chemical or biological weapons. However, it was not until the late 1970s and early 1980s that terrorists began to show an interest in acquiring and using them.

BIOLOGICAL AGENTS

The use of biological weapons has been recorded throughout history. During the fourteenth century, embattled city defenders in Europe and Asia sometimes fought off their besiegers by flinging the bodies of bubonic plague victims over the city walls. In doing so, they spread disease among the attackers and sometimes saved their towns. While colonizing North America, the English intentionally exposed Native Americans to blankets and other items infected with smallpox. The tribes had no immunity to illnesses brought from Europe, so the disease spread quickly. These are examples of early and crude forms of biological warfare—the use of disease, bacteria, or toxins resulting from natural processes against a population.

Agents used in biological warfare fall into five distinct categories: bacteria, viruses, toxins, fungi, and rickettsia. Bacteria are living organisms capable of surviving and reproducing outside a host, sometimes indefinitely. Outbreaks of disease occur when bacteria come into contact with a host. Anthrax, smallpox, and plague are the bacteria most commonly considered for use as weapons.

Viruses are a collection of genes wrapped around a protein, but are not living organisms. Viruses cannot live for long outside a host, which limits the usefulness of some of the most deadly viruses such as encephalitis and yellow fever.

Toxins are chemicals produced by living organisms. They are not alive themselves and cannot reproduce or be spread from person

Emergency workers, dressed in full protective suits, decontaminate a Tokyo, Japan, subway station following a biological terror attack on March 20, 1995. The coordinated attack was carried out on five trains by ten men who released a poisonous gas called sarin. The attack caused widespread fear in a country that has a very low crime rate.

al. Height 2-3 m   This is
s of tropical
e and
s ver
insi
NAT   ays.
NIN   seeds are very poisonous
from children.

The castor bean is used to make castor oil, a laxative which is also used as an ingredient in lubricants, soaps, and varnishes. It is highly toxic because it contains the poison ricin, which can be extracted for use as a biological weapon. Even the leaves and bark of the castor bean plant are toxic.

to person. However, they are extremely poisonous. This category includes venom from insects and reptiles, the highly fatal botulism derived from the *Clostridium botulinum* bacterium, and ricin, a poison extracted from castor bean plants.

Most fungi considered for biological weapons are not directly dangerous to humans. They are generally used to wreck harvests by wiping out crops. Examples include rice blast, which damages rice plants, or coffee rust, which targets coffee trees.

Rickettsia are highly infectious parasitic microorganisms. Though rarely deadly, they spread rapidly and cause a highly infectious and incapacitating disease called Q fever.

CHEMICAL WEAPONS

Chemical agents can either be made in a laboratory or refined from naturally occurring elements for use in warfare. They cannot spread from person to person, but must be carried through the air, water, food supplies, or soil. For a chemical to be useful as a weapon, it has to be highly toxic per unit of weight, resistant to the atmosphere, and easy to manufacture or refine in large quantities.

There are two general kinds of chemical agents. The first set damages body areas that come into contact with them. The second group attacks the nervous system. The first category is the broader of the two and includes three main subtypes: blister agents, choking and incapacitating agents, and blood agents.

Blister agents damage any body surfaces they come into contact with, including skin, eyes, and lungs. Mustard gas in its various forms

CHEMICAL WARFARE IN HISTORY

Chemical weapons have a history dating back to the Peloponnesian War, fought between the ancient Greek city-states of Athens and Sparta (431–404 BC). The ancient Greek historian Thucydides noted that Sparta's army used arsenic smoke against the Athenian city of Delium in 423 BC. Later armies only sporadically employed similar tactics, using foul-smelling or toxic smoke to slow pursuers or overwhelm defenders. The widespread development and use of chemical weapons did not occur until World War I, during which all major powers involved eventually used chemical weapons in gas form. In the decades since World War I, there have been only a handful of confirmed cases of military use of chemical weapons, most notably by Italy in Ethiopia (1935–1936), by Japan in China (1937–1945), by Egypt in Yemen (1963–1967), and by Iraq in Kurdistan and Iran (1983–1988).

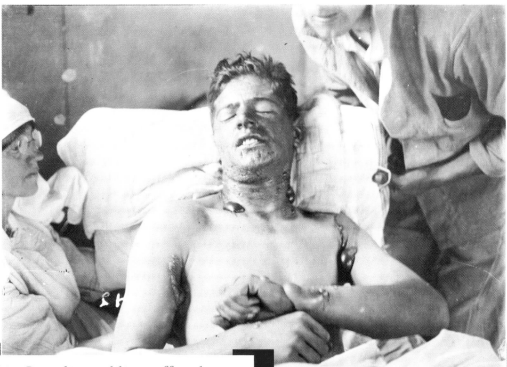

This Canadian soldier suffered mustard gas burns during World War I. Mustard gas causes severe blisters and, if inhaled, can damage the lungs and other organs. Symptoms of exposure to mustard gas appear between one to six hours after exposure.

is a blister agent. Choking and incapacitating agents such as chlorine and phosgene attack the respiratory system. Blood agents such as hydrogen cyanide affect the way oxygen is carried through the bloodstream.

Nerve agents attack the nervous system. They block nerve messages from reaching their intended destination and ultimately cause the body to shut down. Nerve agents can act very rapidly and include deadly chemicals such as sarin and VX.

The symptoms and effects of exposure to chemical weapons vary widely. Nerve agents bring on breathing difficulties, twitching, and convulsions, and ultimately result in coma. Blister agents cause burning sensations in the eyes, blisters, nausea, and an accelerated heart rate. Choking and incapacitating agents irritate the eyes and throat and cause the victim to gasp for breath while the lungs fill with fluid. Blood agents bring on confusion, dizziness, and convulsions as they shut down a victim's respiratory and circulatory systems. Ultimately, any of the three types of chemical weapons can kill.

TERRORISTS AND CHEMICAL AND BIOLOGICAL WEAPONS

There have been very few confirmed instances of the use of chemical or biological weapons in warfare since World War I. By the end of that conflict, all of the major powers had used chemical weapons in gas form, including chlorine, phosgene, and mustard gas. Though it is difficult to gauge how many soldiers were killed by poisonous gas, millions of survivors who had been exposed were debilitated for life as a result.

The effects of these weapons appalled the international community. In 1925, many nations joined together to sign an agreement called the Geneva Protocol, banning the use of poison gas and bacteriological agents in warfare. Later international agreements broadened the Geneva Protocol's Prohibition of the Use in War of Asphyxiating, Poisonous, or Other Gases, and of Bacteriological Methods of Warfare.

The Biological Weapons Convention opened for signatures on April 10, 1972, and went into effect March 26, 1975. It prohibits nations from developing, producing, acquiring, transferring, and using biological agents and toxins. It does not, however, include measures for verifying compliance. Since 1972, 140 nations have signed and ratified the agreement, while 18 others have signed but not ratified it.

The Chemical Weapons Convention is an agreement prohibiting the development, production, acquisition, stockpiling, and use of chemical weapons. It builds upon the Geneva Protocol's prohibition of the use of poisonous gases. It opened for signatures on January 13, 1993, but did not go into effect until April 29, 1997. One hundred and twelve nations have signed and ratified the Chemical Weapons Convention, while fifty-six others have only signed the agreement. It states that all parties must destroy their chemical weapons and facilities for producing them. Unlike the Biological Weapons Convention,

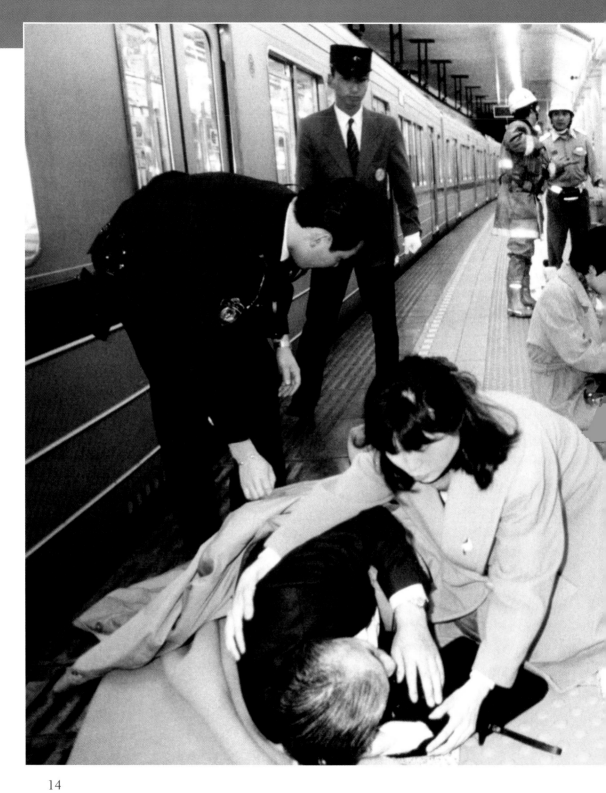

it requires inspections of facilities where chemical weapons were processed or stored. When a nation is suspected of having chemical weapons, the Chemical Weapons Convention allows for the inspection of suspect sites on short notice.

By the end of the twentieth century, most of the world's governments had at least signed the two weapons conventions. However, international law can regulate only governments. Terrorist organizations pay no heed to laws or treaties.

The panic and paranoia these weapons of mass destruction inspire make them highly desirable to terrorists. There have been only a few confirmed instances of terrorists actually using chemical or biological weapons against a population, though there have been many more cases in which groups or individuals were caught with these weapons.

Emergency workers tend to victims of the sarin nerve gas attack on the Tokyo subway system. The attack killed twelve people and injured more than 6,000. The United States is not immune to such an attack. The inset photograph shows canisters of sarin gas at the Blue Grass Army Depot in Richmond, Kentucky, where nearby residents have called for increased security at the facility.

One of the earliest such cases occurred in 1972, when an American neo-Nazi group called the Order of the Rising Sun was caught with large quantities of the bacterium *Typhoid bacillus*. The group planned to taint the water supplies of several Midwest cities, in order to start a typhoid epidemic. In 1986, an American survivalist group called the Covenant, the Sword, and the Arm of the Lord was caught in possession of a thirty-gallon drum of cyanide, with which it had intended to taint water supplies. Another group called the Kurdish Workers Party poisoned water tanks at an air force compound in Istanbul, Turkey, with lethal concentrations of the blood agent potassium cyanide. Fortunately, the poison was discovered before the water could have been used.

Other terrorists have succeeded in using chemical and biological weapons. In 1984, the Rajneeshee cult poisoned salad bars in central Oregon restaurants with the bacteria *Salmonella typhimurium* in an attempt to influence the outcome of a local election. Seven hundred and fifty-one people became ill from food poisoning. It took authorities almost a year to connect the cult with the poisonings.

The most successful and frightening use of chemical or biological weapons by terrorists occurred in 1995, when a Japanese doomsday cult called Aum Shinrikyo released sarin gas in a busy Tokyo subway station. The group, led by a charismatic man named Shoko Asahara, had been experimenting with chemical and biological weapons for years. It recruited scientists and even built an immense laboratory for their research and development.

The group made several failed attempts to use biological weapons throughout the early 1990s. This included an effort to spray botulism toxin on American military bases in 1990 and attempts to spread anthrax throughout Tokyo in 1993. It had more success using chemical weapons. In 1994, the group sent a cloud of sarin gas over the Japanese mountain resort of Matsumoto, killing 7 people and sickening 200 more. The attack was only a test run, and terrorists were not even suspected of the deadly poisoning until much later.

On March 20, 1995, Aum Shinrikyo staged a major attack in Tokyo. Cult members placed sarin-filled plastic pouches on subway cars and

These images are from an Al Qaeda training video that was confiscated in Afghanistan. They show a dog dying after inhaling a white gas that was pumped into its cage. Intelligence officials assert that the videotape provides further evidence of Al Qaeda's interest in acquiring or developing chemical and biological weapons.

then punctured them with sharpened umbrella tips, allowing the gas to escape. The gas killed 12 people and injured more than 6,000 others. The attack horrified the Japanese people, exposing their society as vulnerable to terrorism.

Two similar attempts by cult members were foiled in the months that followed, as Aum Shinrikyo's leaders were arrested, questioned, and put on trial. During the investigation, authorities discovered that the cult had been planning other massive attacks, some in the United States. Their extensive arsenal of chemical and biological weapons included a canister containing enough VX nerve gas to kill 15,000 people. On February 27, 2004, Shoko Asahara became the twelfth member sentenced to death for Aum Shinrikyo's crimes. As of this writing, none of the sentences has been carried out, and Asahara is currently appealing the verdict.

The Aum Shinrikyo case alarmed the world. No other terrorist group had ever developed the sophisticated labs necessary for producing chemical and biological weapons. In November 1998, the CIA confirmed that Osama bin Laden and his Al Qaeda terrorist organization had attempted on several occasions to develop or obtain chemical and biological weapons, including VX gas and sarin.

The September 11 terrorist attacks increased fears that Al Qaeda could acquire and use such weapons. Soon after the attacks, at least four letters containing anthrax spores were mailed to government officials and media figures in the United States. Twenty-three people contracted anthrax from the mailings, five of whom died. Many initially blamed Al Qaeda, but FBI experts believe that an American scientist not connected to Al Qaeda was behind the mailings. Intelligence officials do not know if Al Qaeda possesses chemical or biological weapons. However, an unfinished laboratory found in Afghanistan may have been intended for producing them. U.S. forces also found documents and videos that indicate Al Qaeda was testing chemical weapons on animals. ■

A member of the New Mexico National Guard's Weapons of Mass Destruction Civil Support Team examines a briefcase containing a dummy "dirty bomb" during a mock terrorist event in Alamogordo, New Mexico, in May 2003. WMD Civil Support Teams have been set up in National Guard units across the country to assist civil authorities to respond to a domestic weapons of mass destruction incident.

THE DIRTY BOMB: CONSTRUCTION, DEPLOYMENT, AND CONSEQUENCES

Most experts on terrorism agree that it would be extremely difficult for a terrorist organization to construct a nuclear bomb, the most destructive and universally feared weapon known. The time and expertise needed to build a nuclear bomb, not to mention acquiring the necessary materials, technology, and scientific personnel, make it very difficult even for developed nations to create nuclear weapons. Even the possibility of terrorists stealing a nuclear weapon or purchasing one on the black market without being detected is an unlikely scenario.

During the mid-1990s, Al Qaeda made many attempts to purchase nuclear materials, and its leader Osama bin Laden declared that he had a nuclear weapon in November 2001. U.S. officials dismissed his statement. However, documents found in Afghanistan indicate that bin Laden actively sought a nuclear weapon. Experts, therefore, take the faint possibility of terrorists acquiring nuclear weapons very seriously.

A more likely threat is that terrorists may gather together enough low-grade radioactive material to build a radiation-dispersal device (RDD), ominously known to most people as a dirty bomb.

THE DIRTY BOMB AND NUCLEAR WEAPONS

Though dirty bombs and nuclear weapons both use radioactive material, there is a significant difference between the two. Both types of weapons rely on radioactive material, but a nuclear weapon's destructive power comes from a nuclear reaction, brought about when atoms of certain radioactive elements such as uranium 235 or plutonium are split in a process called fission. In nuclear weapons, fission results in a powerful nuclear explosion characterized by heat intense enough to destroy buildings and vaporize victims.

Fission does not take place when a dirty bomb goes off, so its explosive power is significantly less than that of a nuclear bomb. Because no nuclear reaction takes place, the radioactive material used for dirty bombs can be of a lower quality than that used in nuclear weapons. Terrorists would need about 75 pounds (34 kilograms) of weapons-grade uranium to build a sophisticated nuclear weapon and 120 pounds (54.4 kg) for a crude nuclear weapon. Far less material is required to build a dirty bomb.

The refining process for both types of fissile material, uranium 235 and plutonium, is dangerous, expensive, and time-consuming. Terrorists would also have to build the necessary facilities, obtain equipment, hire scientists, and acquire the raw material for a nuclear weapon. A terrorist organization wishing to keep its intentions secret while

Radiation safety employees check barrels of low-level commercial nuclear waste at the Hanford Site in Washington State, where the U.S. Department of Energy stores the nuclear waste in underground trenches. In recent years, governments all over the world have been boosting security personnel and procedures at nuclear waste sites to prevent terrorists and other criminals from gaining access to these dangerous materials.

Enriched uranium 235 is used as fuel inside nuclear reactors and as an explosive in nuclear weapons. This button of enriched uranium 235, which weighs 11 pounds (5 kg) is worth approximately $200,000.

building a nuclear weapon would have very little chance of success.

If terrorists wished to acquire a nuclear weapon, they could avoid the expense and danger of acquiring fissionable materials by stealing one from a storage facility. In that case, even if they managed to thwart security, the theft would likely be detected and international security forces would move swiftly to arrest the culprits. Terrorists would have a much easier time building a dirty bomb.

BUILDING A DIRTY BOMB

The Council on Foreign Relations, an American research center, estimates that it would take at least twelve highly skilled scientists to develop a nuclear weapon. Compared with constructing a nuclear weapon, building a dirty bomb requires very little scientific knowledge.

A dirty bomb consists of a conventional explosive device packed with radioactive material. It can be made with any radioactive material, from weapons-grade uranium to hospital waste. When the explosive detonates, it disperses the radioactive material around the site of the blast. No fission chain reaction takes place, so the force of the explosion is only as strong as the explosive device itself.

Any type of radioactive material would serve to build a dirty bomb. However, terrorists would likely prefer weapons-grade uranium or plutonium in order to make these devices more destructive. Since the device disperses radiation by exploding and spewing radioactive debris through the air, terrorists would not have to worry about finding the means to launch a missile or drop a bomb. The explosive core could be as large as a truck bomb or as small as a stick of dynamite.

The biggest obstacle for terrorists seeking to build and use a dirty bomb lies in gathering the materials. Though they would not have to worry about refining uranium or making plutonium, radioactive materials are still difficult to obtain. In theory, high quantities of the radioactive isotopes needed for a dirty bomb can be found in many places, including hospitals, industrial plants, and waste from nuclear power plants. Nearly every country in the world has facilities that work with radioactive material.

Though the science is crude, the risk is still great for the bomb maker. A terrorist working with plutonium, uranium, or spent fuel rods could easily be killed just attempting to fasten the materials together. Working with more stable materials such as hospital waste is less risky, but the bomb maker still runs the risk of exposure to radiation.

USING A DIRTY BOMB

No terrorist organization has ever used a dirty bomb. Al Qaeda operatives have attempted to build one, but there has been no evidence that they have succeeded. Since dirty bombs have never been used, many of the effects suggested by experts remain hypothetical.

Once a terrorist group has built a dirty bomb, the question of how and where to use it arises. Terrorists equipped with a dirty bomb

Crude radiation bomb

A "dirty" radiation bomb is far easier to build than a true nuclear at

Radiation dispersion bomb ('dirty bomb')

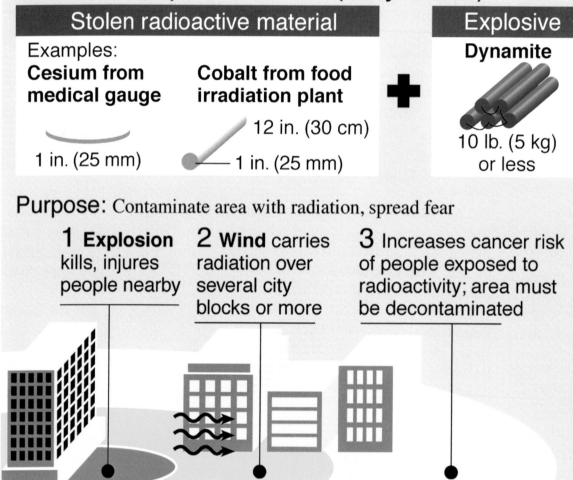

Stolen radioactive material	Explosive
Examples:	**Dynamite**
Cesium from medical gauge **Cobalt from food irradiation plant**	
12 in. (30 cm)	
1 in. (25 mm) 1 in. (25 mm)	10 lb. (5 kg) or less

Purpose: Contaminate area with radiation, spread fear

1 Explosion kills, injures people nearby

2 Wind carries radiation over several city blocks or more

3 Increases cancer risk of people exposed to radioactivity; area must be decontaminated

Source: Journal of the Federation of American Scientists, "The Making of the Atomic Bomb" by Richard Rhodes, U.S. Centers for Disease Control and Prevention, KRT Photo Service   G

mb. A comparison:

sion bomb (atomic bomb)
s expensive, sophisticated parts

Ultra-precise circuit
iggers blast

Shaped
xplosive
ompresses
ore

Plutonium
r uranium 235
xplodes in nuclear chain reaction

pose:
roy target
explosion

erful blast,
ation kill
isands; bomb
ites cloud of
oactive dust,
'allout"

© 2002 KRT

would want to cause as much damage as possible to the target area while alarming the population. For maximum impact, it is likely that they would deploy the device in a city's downtown or commercial district.

A dirty bomb's effectiveness is largely determined by the size of the bomb itself and the type and amount of radioactive material used. Refined uranium, plutonium, and spent nuclear fuel rods would be the most devastating. Medical waste such as radium or cesium isotopes used in cancer treatments would be less harmful, but still hazardous. Terrorists can make a crude dirty bomb with as little as a few ounces of radioactive medical waste wrapped around a small explosive. This flexibility would allow terrorists to choose their targets carefully, to maximize

This diagram illustrates the differences between a dirty bomb and a nuclear bomb. It emphasizes that the relative ease of constructing a dirty bomb makes it a practical goal for terrorist organizations.

THE CASE OF JOSE PADILLA

On May 8, 2002, police at Chicago's O'Hare Airport arrested a man named Jose Padilla after receiving a tip from suspected Al Qaeda leader Abu Zubaydah. Padilla had just flown into the airport from Pakistan under the name Abdullah al-Muhajir, allegedly to do reconnaissance in preparation for detonating a dirty bomb. Padilla, a former street gang member, had converted to Islam while serving a prison term in Florida during the mid-1990s. After his release in 1998, Padilla traveled to Afghanistan, where he met Abu Zubaydah in 2001. Zubaydah sent Padilla to Pakistan, where he allegedly met with other Al Qaeda officials and learned how to make dirty bombs. Authorities say that the plot was in its early stages and that a target had not yet been chosen, though Washington,

This photograph of Jose Padilla, wearing a red scarf, was taken at the Darcel Uloom Islamic Institute in Florida between 1995 and 1997.

D.C., and Chicago were both possibilities. Since his arrest, Padilla has been declared an enemy combatant, held without charges in a naval prison in South Carolina. It is still unclear why Zubaydah told authorities about Padilla. However, it is possible that he wanted to alarm the United States with the knowledge that Al Qaeda had successfully recruited an American citizen.

the effect. Bombs could be carried into busy government buildings or monuments in a briefcase, driven into parking garages in downtown business or entertainment districts, or smuggled into busy ports packed in shipping containers.

After World War II ended in 1945, the U.S. government conducted studies on the possibility of developing radiation-dispersal devices for military use. The tests revealed several reasons why dirty bombs would be impractical for military use. Though the material used for dirty bombs would probably not be as volatile and dangerous as refined weapons-grade uranium or plutonium, they would still generate a great deal of heat and require expensive shielding prior to detonation. Some radioactive materials decay very quickly. They would have to be rushed into use, increasing the possibility of mistakes and failure. If the bomb were used in a downtown area dominated by tall buildings, much of the radiation would be absorbed into the buildings, therefore limiting its dispersal and effectiveness.

The various drawbacks that discouraged the United States from developing radiation-dispersal devices are of only limited concern to determined terrorists. Terrorists would want their dirty bombs to cause as much damage as possible, but alarming the general public would likely remain their primary goal. This frees them from the military's tactical concerns about tall buildings trapping radiation or a lack of wind to help it spread.

EFFECTS OF A DIRTY BOMB

During the Cold War, the possibility of the United States and the Soviet Union entering a full-scale nuclear war seemed very real. Fallout shelters—underground spaces equipped with food and other supplies where people could theoretically wait out the aftermath of nuclear war—began appearing in public places. People of all walks of life took note of instructions on how to prepare for a nuclear attack. The harmful effects of exposure to radiation became well-known to people all over the world. Global tensions eased when the Cold War ended in 1991 as a result of the breakup of the Soviet Union.

However, the dangers posed by nuclear weapons and radiation are difficult to forget.

These fears, established and strengthened by the Cold War, play directly into the hands of terrorists determined to detonate a dirty bomb. Technically, four factors determine the destructive power of a dirty bomb: the type of radioactive material used, the amount packed around the explosive, the size of the explosion itself, and the distance that the radioactive material spreads. People near the bomb at the time of detonation would likely be killed or hurt by the force of the explosion itself. Many of the injured would likely die of radiation sickness in the following weeks.

When a dirty bomb goes off, the initial damage is caused by the explosive device itself. Conventional explosions cause damage through the rapid expansion of very hot gas. A dirty bomb uses the gas expansion to propel radioactive materials through the air in a cloud. Available winds then carry the radioactive debris outward to cover a much larger area.

Unless officials somehow obtain warning of its radioactive nature, an exploding dirty bomb would likely appear to be a conventional explosive. Its nature would only become known once experts arrive on the scene with radiation detectors. The radioactive materials packed around the explosive would disperse, blending with dust and debris. Radioactive particles would be inhaled, ingested, or absorbed into wounds by people in the immediate area of the explosion. Contact would lead to possible damage to organs and tissues, as well as an increased cancer risk.

The radioactive isotopes would cause illnesses and health problems through ionizing radiation, which is radiation with enough strength to knock an electron off an atom. Within the human body, atoms are balanced between positively charged protons and electrons carrying negative charges. When the ionizing radiation causes an atom to lose an electron, it also loses this balance. The atom develops an electrical charge, becoming an ion. The electron that had been lost may then collide with another atom, creating another ion.

Officials watch emergency workers and actors posing as victims during a mock dirty bomb attack in Seattle, Washington, on May 12, 2003. The exercise is part of a series staged by the U.S. Department of Homeland Security to provide training for federal, state, and local officials and emergency workers for responding to a weapons of mass destruction attack.

These ions can cause problems within the body because their electrical charges can result in unnatural chemical reactions within cells. Ions may cause deoxyribonucleic acid (DNA) chains within cells to break, causing the affected cells to mutate, malfunction, or die. When too many cells die, the immune system begins to break down and the body becomes more susceptible to disease. Mutated cells can become cancerous, causing cancer to eventually spread throughout the body. Malfunctioning cells result in a variety of symptoms referred to collectively as radiation sickness.

Many victims of a dirty bomb would show signs of suffering from radiation sickness in the following weeks. Some symptoms would last for as long as several months, depending on the degree of exposure. Those with light exposure might not show any short-term signs of illness, while slightly greater exposure would cause only temporary nausea and vomiting. More severe radiation sickness results in nausea, hair loss, and a weakened immune system. The worst cases of radiation poisoning would result in hemorrhaging, severe dehydration, anemia, and infections, likely to kill 80 to 100 percent of victims.

The level of exposure necessary for such severe radiation sickness is extremely unlikely in the case of a dirty bomb. Over time, cancer cases near the area of detonation could increase, but only slightly. Though lives would be lost, the majority of victims would likely recover.

The primary damage caused by a dirty bomb would be psychological and economic. Direct physical damage would be limited to the site of the explosion. However, the area would have to undergo a long and expensive cleanup process before becoming safe for people. It would take months or even years and potentially cost billions of dollars.

If the explosion occurred in a business or commercial district, the entire area would likely be off-limits for the duration of the cleanup, costing the local economy even more money. Buildings would have to be scrubbed and topsoil removed to alleviate the public's fears. Hospitals would fill up with people ill from radiation sickness. As news of a dirty bomb explosion spread, people would likely panic over the possibility of radiation sickness, disrupting lives across the country. Even after completing the cleanup, many people would continue avoiding the area from fear of radiation, thus perpetuating the damage caused by the bomb for years to come.

Radiation-dispersal devices are not prohibited by any international treaty such as those that ban biological and chemical weapons. However, the difficulties in acquiring materials and successfully assembling and then smuggling a dirty bomb past vigilant security personnel to its intended destination still make the possibility of such an attack remote. ■

3
TERRORIST GROUPS AND THEIR POTENTIAL ACCESS TO WMD

During the second half of the twentieth century, many of the world's weapons of mass destruction were controlled by the United States, the Soviet Union, and their respective allies. The two superpowers kept careful surveillance on each other, assuring that neither nation would gain the chemical, biological, or nuclear edge that would upset the delicate balance of power and plunge the world into war. As decades passed, the two nations gradually began to work together to lessen the threat of such a disaster.

When the Soviet Union finally collapsed in 1991, many hoped for an era of peace, free of the proliferation of weapons of mass destruction. Unfortunately, dreams of a future without fear of these weapons disintegrated quickly. Developing nations emerged as potential threats to world peace, armed with weapons of mass destruction. More seriously, terrorists began showing a real interest in developing chemical, biological, and radiological weapons. In 1995, the Aum Shinrikyo sarin attack demonstrated that terrorists were capable of acquiring and using weapons of mass destruction with devastating consequences.

RUSSIA'S SECURITY NIGHTMARE

Once the Cold War ended, developing nations stepped up their weapons programs, ready to assert themselves on the world stage. The Soviet Union, once a superpower consisting of many nations, fragmented completely. Many of its member states became independent. When these nations gained independence, Soviet military arsenals, laboratories, and weapons knowledge came under the control of newly independent nations, including Russia, Belarus, Kazakhstan, the Ukraine, Georgia, and others. Security at weapons storage facilities quickly became an international concern. However, to this day many of the former Soviet states remain very poor and funds for security are scarce.

Much of the world's fear concerning security in the former Soviet Union focuses on nuclear sites. Russia bought back or disarmed all of the USSR's nuclear weapons by 1996 but took no steps to clean up or secure nuclear power plants and dump sites for radioactive waste. The financial crises in many of the former Soviet republics continue to severely undermine attempts at security. Deteriorating security increases the chance that terrorists interested in building dirty bombs

Nuclear workers deactivate and dismantle nuclear weapons at an unidentified location in Russia on January 1, 1995. For many years after the collapse of the Soviet Union, disgruntled workers and lax security at nuclear facilities in former Soviet states have contributed to an illegal market for nuclear materials. This market provides a likely source for terrorists seeking weapons of mass destruction.

A nuclear rocket is paraded through Moscow in November 1967, during a celebration marking the fiftieth anniversary of the October Revolution, when Bolsheviks took power in Russia. The Soviet Union developed an impressive arsenal of nuclear weapons during the Cold War. Today, terrorists seek to tap into its bountiful store of nuclear materials and wastes, much of which are not adequately secured.

could acquire the necessary radioactive material. Scientists and guards who work around radioactive material are very poorly paid, which increases the odds of a terrorist group successfully bribing its way into a nuclear facility.

The old Soviet Union's nuclear weapons have either been destroyed or moved into Russia. However, that does not necessarily make them more secure. Low pay and payroll shortfalls within Russia's armed forces have led to widespread corruption. This increases the danger that members of the Russian military itself could begin smuggling nuclear weapons and radioactive material for dirty bombs and selling them to other nations or terrorist groups.

As early as February 1993, Russia reported that uranium had been stolen from its facilities three times in two years. Since then, reports of such thefts have increased dramatically. Most of these cases have involved nonfissile radioactive materials, likely intended for dirty bombs. Thefts of radioactive waste useful in making dirty bombs such as low-grade uranium, cesium 137 (a by-product of nuclear fission used in industrial and medical research), or cobalt 60 (a radioactive isotope used in manufacturing to detect flaws in metal parts) have occurred frequently enough to induce worry within the international community.

Smuggling cases involving highly enriched weapons-grade uranium have also arisen. Since the initial Russian report of smugglers trying to acquire uranium, there have been twenty more attempts. Discouragingly, these cases often involve security or military personnel. In August 1994, corrupt Russian Foreign Service Intelligence agents attempted to smuggle nearly 1 pound (0.5 kg) of radioactive plutonium oxide from Moscow to Munich, Germany. An episode in 1998 involved a conspiracy among employees within Russia's Chelyabinsk-65 nuclear weapons production facility. The workers allegedly attempted to steal 44 pounds (20 kg) of highly enriched uranium, possibly enough to produce a small nuclear bomb or dozens of dirty bombs. The thieves were arrested before they left the facility.

Russia's security problems continue to worsen as it works to dismantle its nuclear arsenal, placing more dangerous radioactive material in

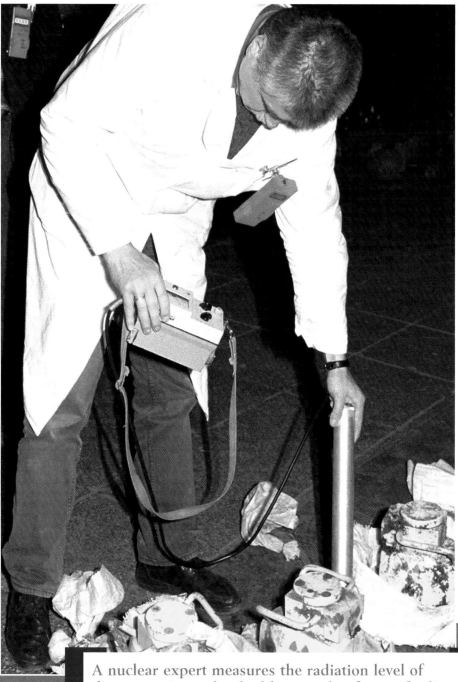

A nuclear expert measures the radiation level of three containers that had been stolen from a facility in Russia's Sverdlovsk region. The thieves were arrested by the local police as they attempted to sell the dangerous materials. The gamma radiation levels of the packages exceeded the standard safe rate by 2,000 times.

sometimes poorly secured storage facilities. Following the September 11 attacks, the United States has raised concerns about Russia's security in light of recent smuggling incidents involving weapons-grade radioactive material. As recently as November 2001, there have been reports from the Russian military of attempts to break into nuclear storage facilities.

In a report to Congress issued on February 22, 2002, the United States Central Intelligence Agency (CIA) expressed concerns about nuclear smuggling from Russia. It said: "We assess that undetected smuggling has occurred, although we do not know the magnitude of such thefts. Nevertheless we are concerned about the total amount of material that could have been diverted over the last ten years." While Russia willingly acknowledges that attempts have been made to smuggle nuclear and radioactive materials from its facilities, it denies that any such substances have disappeared.

TERRORISTS AND RADIOACTIVE MATERIALS

Russia's nuclear security problems are the most prominent in the world. However, security holes are possible at nuclear facilities all over the world. There are over 30,000 nuclear warheads and bombs held between the nuclear powers: the United States, Russia, China, India, Pakistan, France, Israel, and Great Britain. In addition, there are over 450 tons of plutonium and 1,700 tons of highly enriched uranium stockpiled globally. Another three tons of enriched uranium sits in research reactors worldwide. It is unlikely that terrorists could build even crude nuclear weapons from enriched radioactive materials. However, the possibility of using them in dirty bombs makes them a tempting target.

Osama bin Laden, Al Qaeda's leader, has tried for years to attain radioactive and nuclear material. According to the CIA, he was presented with a metal container reportedly holding radioactive material at a meeting in Afghanistan in 2001. Another report states that in December of 2001, U.S. military personnel had found traces of radioactive uranium 238 in a series of tunnels near Kandahar, Afghanistan. If true, the allegation that Jose Padilla was part of an Al Qaeda plot to use

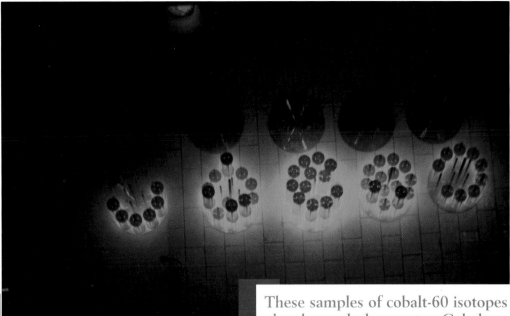

These samples of cobalt-60 isotopes glow beneath deep water. Cobalt (including cobalt-60) is a hard, brittle blue-gray metal. It is used in many medical tests and treatments, and in various industrial applications, such as leveling devices.

a dirty bomb in an American city only confirms the organization's interest in radiological weapons.

Unfortunately, terrorists in the United States would not have to worry about smuggling radioactive materials into the country. The Nuclear Regulatory Commission in the United States licenses 21,000 organizations to use radioactive devices in industry, health care, and research. The commission estimates that among these organizations, 300 radiation sources are lost, stolen, or abandoned each year. The most frequently missed of these items are isotopes of cesium, americium, iridium, and cobalt, all useful in the production of dirty bombs.

Internationally, there have been 175 cases of smugglers trafficking in nuclear material and another 201 incidents involving other radioactive sources since 1993. The increase in smuggling nuclear and radioactive substances can be partially attributed to the deterioration of the security infrastructure in the former Soviet Union, as well as relaxation of security standards in the United States since the end of the Cold War. The biggest reason smuggling has been so prevalent is the sheer increase in nuclear material, most of it intended for peaceful purposes. In addition to all of the world's nuclear weaponry, there are 438 nuclear power reactors, 651 nuclear reactors used for research purposes, and 250 fuel cycle plants designed to process, convert, enrich, and store nuclear materials worldwide.

Another potential way for terrorists to create chaos using radioactive materials would be to sabotage a nuclear facility. Experts from the International Atomic Energy Authority (IAEA), an organization within the United Nations established to promote nuclear safety and peace, feel that the danger from nuclear sabotage would be far greater than the effects of a dirty bomb.

The IAEA estimates that terrorists could cause over 100,000 deaths by sabotaging a nuclear power plant and dispersing intensely radioactive material. An accident at the Three Mile Island reactor near Harrisburg, Pennsylvania, in 1979 exposed the expense and danger of a nuclear accident to the American people. Only a small amount of radioactive gas escaped from the facility, but the incident alarmed the public and the cleanup cost over a billion dollars.

Nuclear power plants in the United States were designed to withstand earthquakes, strong winds, and small aircraft crashing into reactors. Since the September 11 attacks, safety experts worry that similar attacks on a nuclear reactor could create a large-scale disaster. Authorities are still assessing whether or not U.S. nuclear facilities could withstand the deliberate crash of a large, fully fueled jetliner directly into their reactors.

The Nuclear Regulatory Commission requires that all 104 operational nuclear power plants in the United States be protected against three types of terrorist attack. The first scenario involves a small, highly trained group working with information acquired through an accomplice working inside. The second scenario focuses on an insider working alone. The last deals with the possibility of a truck bomb detonating outside the facility. Defenses against these possibilities are tested every eight years using a force of mock intruders. Between 2000 and 2001, tests at six of eleven sites resulted in the simulated disabling of enough equipment to damage reactors. Security at all of these sites has since been upgraded.

AMATEUR NUCLEAR SCIENCE

In 1977, a physics student at Princeton University named John Aristotle Phillips approached his professor, the noted physicist Freeman Dyson, and proposed writing a term paper called "How to Build Your Own Atomic Bomb." In carrying out his research, Phillips consulted declassified documents at the National Technical Information Service. He eventually developed a workable design for a beach ball–sized atomic bomb. Phillips received an A for his work, but the U.S. government classified his paper so that it would not fall into the hands of terrorists or other countries.

More recently, an Eagle Scout named David Hahn developed an interest in nuclear physics. Pretending to be a high-school physics teacher, Hahn wrote letters to the Nuclear Regulatory Commission. The organization sent him information on how to isolate radioactive isotopes. He collected radioactive material from various household objects, conducting his experiments in a shed behind his mother's house. In 1994, at the age of seventeen, Hahn built a small nuclear reactor by mixing his radioactive isotopes and wrapping them with tin foil and duct tape. Alarmed by the amount of radiation he was producing, Hahn took his reactor apart and attempted to dump his material. The local police noticed, bringing in workers from the Environmental Protection Agency and the Nuclear Regulatory Commission. Workers dressed in radiation-proof suits dismantled the shed and sealed its contents and remains into thirty-nine barrels, which they shipped to a nuclear waste storage site.

Cases such as these demonstrate that if students can easily obtain information and materials for nuclear devices, terrorists could replicate their success with devastating results.

This photograph shows steam flowing from the cooling towers of the Three Mile Island nuclear power plant in Middletown, Pennsylvania, on March 28, 1979, after an accident resulted in the production of radioactive gases. Nearby residents were evacuated. Security experts warn that terrorists may target nuclear power plants in the United States.

ACQUIRING CHEMICAL AND BIOLOGICAL WEAPONS

Terrorists could have an easier time obtaining chemical or biological weapons than nuclear or radioactive material, but they would still face formidable obstacles. Chemical weapons would be the easier of the two to acquire. To make some gases, terrorists need little more scientific background than a basic understanding of chemistry. The Japanese doomsday cult Aum Shinrikyo produced massive amounts of poisonous gases, including cyanide, VX nerve gas, and the sarin used in the Tokyo subway attacks.

Terrorists could simply ignore chemistry altogether by using common chemicals, minerals, and substances to poison large numbers of people. Some agricultural or industrial chemicals are very easy to purchase, and it would require little effort to dump them into a city's water supply. Another possibility is the use of toxic heavy metals such as mercury, lead, or arsenic, though it would take large amounts of these materials to have much of an effect on a locality's citizens.

Countries whose governments allegedly support terrorism could hand chemical weapons over to terrorists. Despite the Chemical Weapons Convention, some nations still own and develop chemical weapons. Nations that have not signed the CWC and are suspected of having large chemical weapon stockpiles include North Korea, Syria, and Egypt. The threat imposed by poor security at laboratories in the former Soviet Union is another concern. Though there are no confirmed cases of terrorists trying to steal chemical weapons from Russian labs and storage facilities, the security at those places is no better than around Russia's nuclear sites.

Many of the same scenarios apply to terrorists acquiring biological weapons. In the case of biological weapons, there have been several confirmed thefts from facilities in the former Soviet Union. In recent years, pathogens such as smallpox, anthrax, and the plague have all been either stolen or diverted from research laboratories in Russia, Kazakhstan, and the Republic of Georgia. Scientists working at these facilities are paid very little, again making bribery a very real possibility.

Like chemical weapons, terrorists can easily produce some biological pathogens. In 1999 and 2000, U.S. intelligence agencies secretly carried out an operation called Project BACCHUS to see how easily terrorists could manufacture biological weapons. Officials built a production plant at a remote location in the Nevada desert and produced a number of simulated biological agents using commercially available substances. Considering the ease with which they may be obtained or produced, many weapons experts now believe that it is only a matter of time before another major terrorist strike occurs using chemical or biological weapons. ■

Emergency service teams carry radiation and nerve agent detectors during a weapons of mass destruction drill in New York City on March 14, 2004. Since 9/11, federal, state, and many local governments have stepped up their efforts to equip police, fire, and other emergency services with such devices.

PREVENTING WMD TERRORISM ATTEMPTS

Following the Aum Shinrikyo subway attack, the United States began to take steps making it more difficult for terrorists to acquire and use weapons of mass destruction. The need for greater security became even more apparent following the September 11 attacks. Experts fear that the next terrorist attack

Officials from various federal departments and agencies monitor information coming into a master control center in Arlington, Virginia, during simultaneous terror drills in Washington State and Illinois.

against the United States will involve chemical, biological, or radiological weapons (dirty bombs).

RECENT COUNTERTERRORISM EFFORTS

On June 21, 1995, President Bill Clinton issued counterterrorist guidelines in a document called Presidential Decision Directive 39. The document deals with terrorism in all of its forms but focuses on the dangers posed by biological, chemical, nuclear, and radiological weapons of mass destruction. It states that the United States will not be swayed by terrorist attacks, makes returning indicted terrorism suspects to the United States to face trial a top priority, and outlines the nation's intentions to identify and punish nations and groups that support terrorists.

Presidential Decision Directive 39 also assigns duties to different government agencies to perform in identifying terrorist threats and dealing with the aftermath of an attack. For example, the secretary of state was assigned the task of assessing the vulnerability of nonmilitary government installations and personnel abroad. The secretary of defense was put in charge of reducing the risk of terrorist attacks to the armed forces.

One of the most important tasks under the new guidelines fell to the Central Intelligence Agency. The director of the CIA became responsible for leading the intelligence community in an aggressive program of foreign intelligence gathering, analysis, and response to terrorist threats to American interests worldwide.

Counterterrorist intelligence officials foiled a number of terrorist plots in the following years, but Presidential Decision Directive 39 has been all

PRESIDENTIAL DECISION DIRECTIVE 39

In 1995, President Bill Clinton issued Presidential Decision Directive 39, a document that makes many suggestions for preventing terrorism. Near the end, the directive addresses concerns regarding weapons of mass destruction. "The United States shall give the highest priority to developing effective capabilities to detect, prevent, defeat and manage the consequences of nuclear, biological or chemical materials or weapons use by terrorists. The acquisition of weapons of mass destruction by a terrorist group, through theft or manufacture, is unacceptable. There is no higher priority than preventing the acquisition of this capability or removing this capability from terrorist groups potentially opposed to the U.S." In the wake of the Aum Shinrikyo attack, the possibility that terrorists would again use weapons of mass destruction with even more devastating consequences seemed very real. However, the terrorists who carried out the September 11 attacks six years later relied on simple tactics, improvised weapons, and ingenuity to wreak havoc. By using means other than weapons of mass destruction, they emphasized the unpredictable nature of terrorism and the difficulties involved in preparing for any eventuality.

PROTECTING THE HOMELAND
SEAL OF THE PRESIDENT OF THE UNITED STATES

but forgotten in the wake of the September 11 attacks. Criticism over intelligence failures, particularly a lack of communication between the CIA and the Federal Bureau of Investigation (FBI), led to massive overhauls of both agencies. Personnel assigned to other tasks within the FBI and CIA have since been shuffled to join the counterterrorism efforts.

RESPONDING TO TERRORIST ATTACKS

In November 2002, Congress passed legislation allowing for the creation of a Department of Homeland Security. The agency was designed by the Bush administration to coordinate America's defenses for the possibility, and, if necessary, the aftermath of a terrorist attack. A number of independent agencies were combined to form the Department of Homeland Security, including the Coast Guard, the Secret Service, the Border Patrol,

President Bush *(left)* discusses the creation of a cabinet-level Department of Homeland Security as Director (now Secretary) of Homeland Security Tom Ridge looks on. The Department of Homeland Security combines twenty-two government agencies under one department in order to better coordinate prevention and response to attacks on the United States.

Physicist Mike Dunning demonstrates a new RadScout radiation detector by scanning luggage. RadScout was developed for emergency and inspection personnel who need to quickly detect and identify radioactive material. Radscout was developed at the Department of Homeland Security's Lawrence Livermore National Laboratory in Livermore, California, after the Department of Defense made an urgent call for portable, easy-to-use detectors for screening luggage and shipping containers.

the Customs Service, the Immigration and Naturalization Service, and the Transportation Security Administration. By placing all of these agencies under the control of one department, the government hopes to increase cooperation and communication among them.

The Department of Homeland Security will also carry out some of the directives of another presidential counterterrorism directive, the National Strategy for Homeland Security unveiled by President George W. Bush on July 16, 2002. The document details objectives for combating terrorism, including cutting off terrorist financing, tracking terror suspects to make it easier to apprehend them, and continuing ongoing terrorism investigations and prosecutions.

The National Strategy for Homeland Security also provides detailed response measures in case of a terrorist attack using chemical, biological, nuclear, or radiological weapons of mass destruction. Specifically, it calls for better radiation detectors in public places to prevent the use of a dirty bomb and sensors to detect chemical and biological agents. It also prioritizes the development of vaccines, antimicrobials, antidotes, and decontamination techniques to deal with attacks using these weapons.

The United States has addressed the threat of biological weapons by boosting the health-care system's ability to handle large epidemics and inspections of food and water supplies. A June 2002 bioterrorism law provided more than $4.6 billion for stockpiling vaccines and medicine, enhancing inspections of the food supply, upgrading security of water systems, and improving hospital preparedness. Additional funding has been proposed for the research and production of vaccines and treatments for biological agents such as anthrax, the plague, and botulinum toxin. The United States has also created a system for detecting the release of deadly germs into the air by adapting air-quality monitoring devices to sense the release of viruses and bacteria. These sensors can warn emergency personnel that an attack has taken place within twenty-four hours, possibly before anyone becomes ill.

Since the Aum Shinrikyo attacks, the U.S. government has set aside many millions of dollars each year for training, equipment, and procedures to prepare cities and towns to deal with a chemical weapons

attack. The first emergency personnel on the scene would play a crucial role, since some chemical agents work very quickly. Police, paramedics, and firefighters dressed in protective gear would first try to decontaminate and treat victims with antidotes. Cordoning off the scene to prevent further contamination, they would then try to determine what chemical was used. Severely contaminated victims would then go to the hospital for further treatment.

Work to prevent nuclear and dirty bomb attacks began in 1991, when Russia and the United States signed the Cooperative Threat Reduction Act. The act authorized the U.S. Department of Defense to help former Soviet states destroy, store, and secure radioactive materials. The two nations continue to work on the project, but progress is slow. As of 2003, only 50 out of 650 tons of nuclear material in Russia has been secured.

Domestically, the United States has pushed for tighter security at

A Ukranian defense official examines a nuclear missile that has been slated for dismantling under the Cooperative Threat Reduction Program. The United States has committed hundreds of millions of dollars to dismantling nuclear arsenals in former Soviet states.

privately run nuclear plants and has installed radiation detectors in strategic places such as airports, train stations, downtown areas, and along highways. In the event of a dirty bomb attack, specially trained teams of doctors, scientists, and engineers from the Environmental Protection Agency can be dispatched from anywhere in the country to deal with the situation. Most hospitals now have the equipment and capability to deal with dirty bomb victims.

Since the September 11 attacks, anxiety has increased over the possibility of terrorists acquiring weapons of mass destruction. Events such as Jose Padilla's arrest and materials found in former Al Qaeda strongholds in Afghanistan reinforce these fears. Attempts by terrorists to acquire radioactive materials show that Al Qaeda and other terrorist groups are interested in building dirty bombs. Even though radiation sensors and other security precautions have been implemented in busy areas, determined terrorists may still use their ingenuity to slip through security and use a dirty bomb. Yet there have also been important steps taken to guarantee that in the event that an attack does occur, America's emergency and medical personnel will be prepared. ■

[GLOSSARY]

americium A radioactive element used in medicine.

anemia A medical condition in which a person's blood is low on red blood cells.

anthrax An infectious and usually fatal bacterial disease.

antimicrobials A substance designed to kill harmful microorganisms.

arsenic A poisonous metallic chemical element.

bacteria Microorganisms, some of which produce diseases.

biological weapons Organisms or toxins found in nature that have been developed for use in warfare.

black market Trade in illicit goods.

botulism toxin A bacterial toxin causing acute paralysis, often found in food.

bubonic plague An infectious disease believed to have caused several severe epidemics throughout history.

cesium A radioactive element used in industry and medicine.

chemical weapons Chemicals designed to kill and harm an enemy for military purposes.

chlorine A chemical element which in its purest form appears as a greenish, irritating gas.

Clostridium botulism The bacterium that produces the toxin botulism, which can cause illness or death if untreated.

cobalt A radioactive element with many industrial and medical uses.

Cold War The rivalry between the United States and the Soviet Union, which lasted from 1945 to 1991 and was characterized by the massive expansion of both nations' weapons and armed forces, particularly nuclear weapons.

debilitate To make weak.

deoxyribonucleic acid (DNA) A chemical located in cells and responsible for determining what traits are passed on to future generations.

detonate Cause to explode.

dirty bomb An explosive used to contaminate an area with radioactive waste.

doomsday cult A religious organization that believes that the end of the world is near.

fissile Capable of being split, particularly referring to atoms useful in producing nuclear reactions.

fission A nuclear reaction in which an atom is split, releasing energy.

fuel rod An object containing uranium and designed to produce energy in a nuclear reactor.

Geneva Protocol An early treaty banning the use of chemical and biological weapons.

guillotine A device consisting of a weighted blade between two vertical poles, used for beheading people.

intelligence Information gathered about a threat or an enemy.

iridium A glowing radioactive element once commonly used for painting clock faces.

isotope Any of the forms of a chemical element that differ chiefly in the number of electrons in an atom.

microorganism A living organism so small that it is invisible without a microscope.

mustard gas A toxic gas used in warfare that causes severe blisters and attacks the eyes and lungs.

neo-Nazi A person or group inspired by the racist ideas of Adolf Hitler.

nuclear reactor A device used to maintain and control a nuclear fission chain reaction, usually for the production of energy.

nuclear weapons A weapon that gets its destructive power from a nuclear reaction.

Peloponnesian War A war fought between the ancient Greek city-states of Athens and Sparta from 431 BC to 404 BC.

phosgene A colorless toxic gas that attacks the respiratory system.

plutonium A radioactive element used in making nuclear weapons.

proliferation A rapid spread or increase in number.

Q fever An infectious disease caused by rickettsia that results in fever and severe muscular pain.

radioactive Possessing an unstable and therefore dangerous atomic structure.

ratify To approve formally. In many countries, ratification of an international agreement is the responsibility of the main legislative body or bodies, and not the political leader, such as the president, who signs or authorizes another official to sign the agreement. Therefore, it is not uncommon for a country to sign an agreement, such as the Geneva Protocol, but not formally approve it.

Salmonella typhimurium A bacterium that can cause a variety of illnesses, such as food poisoning.

sarin A highly toxic gas that shuts down the nervous system.

terrorism An act of violence, often upon a civilian target, designed to create fear and bring about political or social change.

toxin Poisonous substances produced naturally by some plants and animals.

typhoid bacillus The bacterium that causes typhoid fever, a contagious and sometimes fatal disease.

uranium A radioactive element used in making nuclear fuels and weapons.

VX gas A deadly poisonous gas that attacks the nervous system, causing the body to shut down.

weapons of mass destruction Weapons capable of killing or injuring many people in a single strike.

yellow fever A viral disease that can result in jaundice, fever, and hemorrhaging.

[FOR MORE]
[INFORMATION]

Federal Emergency Management Agency
500 C Street SW
Washington, DC 20472
(202) 566-1600
Web site: http://www.fema.gov

Federation of American Scientists
1717 K Street NW, Suite 209
Washington, DC 20036
e-mail: fas@fas.org
Web site: http://www.fas.org

United States Environmental Protection Agency
Office of Environmental Information
1200 Pennsylvania Avenue NW
Mail Code 2822-T
Washington, DC 20460
(202) 566-1658
Web site: http://www.epa.gov

WEB SITES

Due to the changing nature of Internet links, the Rosen Publishing Group, Inc., has developed an online list of Web sites related to the subject of this book. This site is updated regularly. Please use this link to access the list:

http://www.rosenlinks.com/lwmd/tdbwmd

[FOR FURTHER]
READING

Campbell, Geoffrey A. *A Vulnerable America: An Overview of National Security*. San Diego: Lucent Books, 2003.

Landau, Elaine. *Osama bin Laden: A War Against the West*. Brookfield, CT: Millbrook Press, Inc., 2002.

Mega Book of Weapons and Warfare: Discover the Most Amazing Weapons on Earth. West Chester, PA: Chrysalis Books, 2003.

Meltzer, Milton. *The Day the Sky Fell: A History of Terrorism*. New York: Random House, 2002.

Pringle, Laurence P. *Chemical and Biological Warfare: The Cruelest Weapons*. Springfield, NJ: Enslow Publishers, Inc., 2000.

Streissguth, Thomas. *Nuclear Weapons: More Countries, More Threats*. Springfield, NJ: Enslow Publishers, Inc., 2000.

[BIBLIOGRAPHY]

BBC. "Profile: Jose Padilla." London, June 11, 2002. Retrieved
    March 10, 2004 (http://news.bbc.co.uk/1/hi/world/americas/
    2037444.stm).

Burrows, William E., and Robert Windrem. *Critical Mass: The
    Dangerous Race for Superweapons in a Fragmenting World*. New
    York: Simon and Schuster, 1994.

Cherkasky, Michael, with Alex Prud'homme. *Forewarned: Why the
    Government Is Failing to Protect Us—and What We Must Do to
    Protect Ourselves*. New York: Ballantine Books, 2003.

Cirincione, Joseph, with Jon B. Wolfsthal and Miriam Rajkumar. *Deadly
    Arsenals: Tracking Weapons of Mass Destruction*. Washington, DC:
    Carnegie Endowment for International Peace, 2002.

Council on Foreign Relations. "Terrorism: Questions and Answers." 2004.
    Retrieved March 10, 2004 (http://www.terrorismanswers.com).

Falk, Richard. *The Great Terror War*. New York: Olive Branch
    Press, 2003.

Federation of American Scientists. "Presidential Decision Directive 39:
    US Policy on Counterterrorism." July 21, 1995. Retrieved March
    10, 2004 (http://www.fas.org/irp/offdocs/pdd39.htm).

Gurr, Nadine, and Benjamin Cole. *The New Face of Terrorism:
    Threats from Weapons of Mass Destruction*. London: I. B. Tauris
    Publishers, 2000.

Hoffman, Bruce. *Inside Terrorism*. New York: Columbia University
    Press, 1998.

Hurley, Jennifer A., ed. *Weapons of Mass Destruction: Opposing
    Viewpoints*. San Diego: Greenhaven Press, 1999.

Hutchinson, Robert. *Weapons of Mass Destruction: The No-Nonsense
    Guide to Nuclear, Chemical and Biological Weapons Today*. London:
    Weidenfeld and Nicolson, 2003.

Lee, Rensselear. "Nuclear Smuggling from the Former Soviet Union: Threats and Responses." Philadelphia, PA: Foreign Policy Research Institute, April 27, 2001. Retrieved March 10, 2004 (http://www.nyu.edu/globalbeat/nuclear/FPRI042701.html).

Stern, Jessica. *The Ultimate Terrorists*. Cambridge, MA: Harvard University Press, 1999.

United Press International. "U.S. 'Dirty Bomb' Suspect Sees Lawyer." Charleston, SC, March 4, 2004. Retrieved March 10, 2004 (http://washingtontimes.com/upi-breaking/20040304-071752-4834r.htm).

U.S. Department of State. "Bush Unveils National Strategy for Homeland Security." Washington, D.C., July 16, 2002. Retrieved March 10, 2004 (http://usinfo.state.gov/topical/pol/terror/02071604.htm).

[INDEX]

ABOUT THE AUTHOR
Jason Porterfield is a freelance writer who lives in Chicago, Illinois.

PHOTO CREDITS
Cover © Reuters/Corbis; pp. 4-5 © Thomas Hoepker/Magnum Photos; p. 6 © Steve McCurry/Magnum Photos; p. 8 © Corbis Sygma; p. 10 (top) © Custom Medical Stock Photo, (bottom) © Educational Images/Custom Medical Stock Photo; p. 12 National Archives of Canada; pp. 14-15 Fujifotos/The Image Works, (inset) ©AP/Wide World Photos: p. 17 © CNN/Getty Images; p. 19 © Alamogordo Daily News/AP/Wide World Photos; pp. 21, 39 © Roger Ressmeyer/Corbis; pp. 22-23 KRT/NewsCom; pp. 24-25 U.S. Dept of Energy/Science Photo Library; p. 26 © Getty Images; p. 29 © AFP/Getty Images; p. 32 © EPIX/Corbis Sygma; pp. 34-35 © Marc Garanger/Corbis; p. 37 © TASS/Sovfoto; p. 42 © Wally McNamee/Corbis; p. 45 © Chip East/Reuters/Corbis;p. 46 © Alex Wong/Getty Images; pp. 48-49 © Mark Wilson/Getty Images; p. 50 © Justin Sullivan/Getty Images; pp.52-53 AP/Wide World Photos.

Designer: Evelyn Horovicz; Editor: Wayne Anderson; Layout: Thomas Forget; Photo Researcher: Amy Feinberg